Parenting With Love

TIPS FOR RAISING CHILDREN WITH DISABILITIES

Lisa McBride

FREEAIR BOOKS
FREEAIR Books

FREEAIR Books, 2023

This book is dedicated Doris Taylor, my beloved mother.
This book marks the completion of my mother's dream for me!

Contents

Parenting With Love

Tips for Raising Children with Disabilities

1

Introduction

In life, there are many challenges we face, and many times we question ourselves. Sometimes, the challenges look greater than what we can handle. Some of the challenges we face are because of the decisions we make due to what life has given us. Of these challenges, parenthood is one of the most rewarding yet greatest challenges we will ever face. Raising children to be adults who are responsible, respectful, and able to be there for others as well is a challenge that seems impossible at times. For those of us who have faith in God, we want to raise our children to love God and have a relationship with Him. It is a prayer and hope that we set an example for them to follow. If you do not believe in God, you have hope that you will be the parent your child needs. No matter your situation, each parent wants to be the best parent they can be.

But what happens if we have a child with incredible physical or mental challenges? There is an additional challenge in these situations because some children may not be able to grow to be the adults we had hoped for. They may need us more until well into their adulthood. For parents, this causes fears, and for some, those can be overwhelming. For some, it may be something they feel they cannot handle and do not want to raise the child. The strain can be mental, physical, emotional, and monetary. Some say only a special person can raise a child with special needs. I believe God gives us the ability to care for our children no matter their needs.

Let me tell you a little about myself and my beautiful daughters. I am the mother of three daughters. All have some form of mental challenges. My oldest is Ginny, and she has been diagnosed with Schizo-affective, Obsessive-Compulsive Disorder, and Tourette Syndrome. She has a bachelor's degree in English. She is a highly intelligent young lady and has no learning problems. She is an amazing young woman. Ginny can adapt more easily than my other daughters. This means that she can learn new ways to overcome challenges that arise.

My second daughter, Carolyn, was diagnosed with Attention Deficit Disorder at a young age. As she grew up, her diagnosis changed from Attention Deficit Hyperactive Disorder to Bipolar, and finally, Schizo-affective. Due to an early diagnosis, she has been on medications since she was five. This has disadvantages as well as advantages. The biggest advantage is she had assistance her whole life to control the symptoms of her condition. The disadvantage is she has had to have help her whole life in all areas of her life, which has caused her to not be as confident in herself as she should be. My older daughters have had issues with seeing things or hearing voices. These symptoms were not always obvious at first. These symptoms are quiet and can come out of nowhere, it seems.

My youngest is Bobbie Jo. She is dealing with Anxiety and Depression. As she grew up, she saw me going through the same things. Unfortunately, as I did, she had to learn how to get help. As a mother of these incredible women, I have learned how to help each in their needs. I have raised them mostly as a single mother. Even though I was married three times, I was the main person who dealt with my girls.

I never planned to be the mother of three daughters with special needs. One thing I have learned during this time is how to make many mistakes, how to get help when needed, and how to learn from my mistakes. My girls and I learned together in many ways. Lately, my oldest daughter has reminded me of my many mistakes in our talks. This was not to be mean, but to say she knew and still loved me and knew I was trying to be the best mother I could be.

When I was younger, I remember planning my life. I would marry a man with blonde hair, blue eyes, and tall. We were going to have three kids: two girls and one boy. I was going to be a special education teacher specializing in deaf children. I had based my life on a dream referencing a character in a television show. How many of us do that? We see a character in a show or someone we like a lot and think, "What If." Some dreams do come true, and some don't.

But not many of us dream of having children with special needs. We plan on perfect children with ten toes and ten fingers. From the outside, these babies may seem perfect in every way. We cannot see what is going on inside of them. Some special needs are physical needs like cancer, others have mental issues like Attention Deficit Disorder. As our children mature, we start to see things or reactions and are unsure what to think. We wonder if these actions are normal for their age. Sometimes, we think, did God make a mistake?

There was no mistake. God gives us children as a gift of his love for us. When we love each other and want to build a life together, a child is our love visualized. We see ourselves as well as our partner/spouse. Therefore, when we have a child with challenges, we tend to wonder what is wrong with us. Did we make the right decisions in our lives to this point? One of the hardest things to do is not allow these thoughts to control you.

As parents, we are not prepared when we reach this point. Many parents do not want to believe anything is wrong and do nothing until it gets worse. I know for myself and my first husband, we knew something wasn't right and did not get help until my second daughter began school. The teacher advised us that she needed to be tested. That is when we got both of our daughters tested. Even then, we were not prepared to hear that diagnosis. I remember desperately wanting to cry, but I did not because my babies were watching me. Right then, I was questioning whether I could raise these girls. In that office, I was faced with the hardest thing I have ever been given before. There was a lot to learn, and I was aware that these babies needed me to do all I could and get all the help there was to help them through the rest of their lives. I decided to do whatever I needed to help them grow up to be the amazing women

I knew they could be. The process was unknown, but I knew I had to fight for every moment from that day on.

My husband and I had to work together to protect our daughters. My husband was able to help in ways I could not. We did not allow the 'what if' moment to stop us from doing what was needed. They are now all adults, and I made many mistakes, but they are amazing young ladies. I have been blessed to have them in my life. Sometimes, I look back on our lives and think my girls saved me and helped me more than I was able to help them. If you are at the beginning of the journey, I would advise you to keep getting up every day and keep loving your babies.

One main challenge I had initially was finding books that could help me in practical ways. The books I did find were full of long names of diagnoses and codependents of Attention Deficit Disorder. Some books reference diets. But none of these helped me with everyday life. I spoke to many professionals, and that did help, but there were areas they could not help with. Some of these issues were medicines and their bad side effects, the behaviors they could not see, and how we, as parents, can keep going when we give all we have. As for me, I also had issues with depression that increased at times when trying to be the mother my children needed me to be.

When my children were young, my relationship with God was not as close as I wished, and I learned the hard way in many lessons. I felt all alone and like a failure. Looking back, I was doing my best, and as time passed, I learned how to be a better mother. As my relationship with God grew closer, I learned to look at the challenges differently. I hope that if you feel like you cannot do this and depression has taken hold, this book will help you see options and ways to help. Sometimes, the hardest thing to do is to look for help, no matter what area you need. I hope you see that no matter how strong you feel, you need help to help your child through what can sometimes feel like their world is falling apart.

For those families who have faith in God, we are told children are a gift from God, and we need to rely on Him through these challenges. We need to remember God never gives us more than we can handle with His help. Our example will help our children and, hopefully, those who see the challenges we face. Those who hear our testimony or story see how strong we are and how much we love our children and God. This tells a lot about us, and when we give credit to the Lord, it shows where the strength to do what we did came from.

The main thing is knowing we are not alone but always have God with us. This helps me even now when I have new challenges with my daughters. Every day is new, and we must give our babies to God to protect them and show us how to be there for them. To be the parents we were called to be, we need to not look at why or what if but what we can do better tomorrow than we did today.

The main thing I want you to know is that our special children are gifts from God. They teach us how to genuinely love. I was blessed beyond words to be called their mother. I hope you can see your children this way, that this book will help you have everyday answers, and that you can get confidence and know that you were made for raising your children. I will advise how to deal with doctors; it is okay to question what they say or get another doctor. The next chapters will discuss how to help you and your children.

2

~

What If?

When you find out your child has special needs, your thoughts range from, 'Why, Can I do this, and I can't do this.' You may not see the disorder when you look at your baby, no matter what age. All you see is that cute smile and beautiful eyes. All you hear is the little voice laughing or saying I love you, Mom or Dad. This brings you to where I am blessed to have this child in my life. Sometimes, we do not want to deal with these questions. I call these "What If" moments. We have them in all areas of our lives.

From childhood to adulthood, we say what if many times. These times make us who we are from our experiences through life. When we have children, these moments start with whether they will have my hair or eyes or be like our spouse. These thoughts can determine whether our child will be tall, have our spouse smile, or be as stubborn as ourselves or our spouse. When I was pregnant with my first child, I hoped she would look like my husband. Brett, my husband, was part Palestinian. He had olive skin with a darker tone. His eyes were dark brown, and he had dark hair. I have blue eyes and brown hair with a very white skin tone. I was concerned about my baby's health and what was happening, but not as concerned as I should have been. I took care of myself during my pregnancy but did not think of the entire "what-if" possibilities. This may sound very unimportant to some, but to me, that was my hope.

I was incredibly young and never thought I could have a child that was not perfect. Looking back, I was not thinking of all the possibilities that could happen. When I was pregnant with my second child, I was thinking of different things. I was watching everything so much closer. I did not think about the child's appearance except that she would be healthy and have all her toes and fingers. The entire "what-if" questions did not come up because I did not think about them. Parents want their children to be healthy, which is all I want. But we are never truly prepared for the moment our baby is born. Sometimes, we do not see what is hiding behind our baby's eyes. When we look into our baby's eyes and see so many things. We can see our spouse sometimes, as well as our other children. Sometimes, we can see all the love we share with our spouse or partner.

When I look into my grandchildren's eyes, I see God's love for me and the greatest gift I can receive here on earth. A child's eyes show innocence and want to please their parents. My grandson was diagnosed with Autism. I don't see that diagnosis. I see a smart, wonderful child who loves life and gives love without judgment. I could allow my question to stop me from seeing anything but a child struggling to learn and behind those his age. If you asked my daughter Bobbie about Dominic, her son, she would say he is a challenge, but he is loving and caring. He has a smile that will take away any bad day. She tells me she is blessed to have him in her life. She is learning to love a child through many challenges and yet knows that she can with the help she is given.

I am there for her through all of the challenges. She has a support group, and the "what-if" questions do not stop her from getting up every day and doing everything she can for her son. How do you feel about your child? Is your child a burden or a blessing? What do you see when you look into your child's eyes? Do you see the diagnosis or the love? Do the "what if" questions overwhelm you and stop you from doing what is needed every day? The answers to these questions will show where you are and if you are truly dealing with your child and their challenges or if your child is alone in this battle.

What can be hidden behind those eyes can be mental and physical challenges we need to help with daily. These challenges can be physical, as in cancer, or mental, as in Attention Deficit Disorder. Both can not be seen by the physical eye. What we cannot see can change our lives forever. When we are told by a doctor that our baby has any of these challenges, we are not ready, even with them in our family history.

For myself, I was in total shock. I did not know how to act or think. I was in shock and felt like I could not think or know what to do at that moment. I held my babies, thinking I failed them, and wondered how to raise them how they needed to. What do I do next was the thought? Where do I go from there? I was so stunned that everything I knew about parenting went out the door. I was lost, and yet I had to be stronger and support my daughters during what was to come. This left me scared to make a mistake and not sure how to proceed from that moment.

I blamed my husband, who was the carrier of this gene. It was easier to blame him than to face the problem. When we do not want to find an answer to a question or challenge, we blame someone else. If it is not our problem, then we cannot be blamed or must take responsibility for it. The "what if" thoughts can be put aside because we are not required to deal with them. I wondered why and felt sorry for myself for a short time. This was my way of dealing with most situations at that time. Those questions and doubts were there before; I just never wanted to face them.

Have you ever wondered why we ask this question? The reason we do is because we are not certain about ourselves, our situations, or our future. When looking into our child's eyes, we do not always have the confidence to face what we cannot see. Because I was not confident and was overwhelmed, I emotionally held back from my girls for a short time to get myself in control. You must get yourself in control to help your child. This is not always easy; you may have to look at yourself and talk to others to get the "what if" questions out of your way.

I tell my daughters, who are the mothers of my grandchildren, that they have a choice to do all they can to love and help them no matter what. I say to look into their eyes and see the love and not the diagnosis, whatever it may be. When your child may have some form of challenge, let them know the "what if" questions will not stop you from seeing them, not the challenge. Each person is different and will have different reactions.

As parents, I want to show you these emotions and thoughts are normal. The hardest part is working past them and seeing them as they are, moments of doubt in an uncertain situation. We must remember that our children will be facing times of doubt, and we need to be the ones who encourage them and always have their backs. The fact that we are always here will show them that they are important. If we can not get past these doubts, we cannot help them.

So, how did you feel when you were told of our child's diagnosis? How are you feeling now? I can say that even after 35 years of raising my girls, I still have doubts and need to remind myself it is okay not to know all the answers. In the last few years, I learned I still try to have the answers. We all must learn that lesson repeatedly. I do have to tell those what-if questions to go away. Doubts will come and try to tell you that you are not enough. I am a witness to this. You must learn to deal with these doubts when a situation is new or repeated. These questions are not bad for us; hey can help us strive harder to help our children.

Every day, we must be real about who we are and ready to face the person in the mirror. Honesty with ourselves is imperative to face these doubts and our children. If we are not honest, we will end up ineffective in our parenting, whether our child has special needs or not. But for a child with special needs, honesty with who we are is the best way to help them be honest with themselves. They have what-if moments, too. How you deal with yours will guide them in dealing with their own.

I tried to be honest with myself and be the best example for my girls, but I did not know who I was for a long time. Therefore, my girls and I grew up together. This may happen to you as well. You will have renewed doubts and concerns when you go through different situations. The journey has many bumps and turns, so we are unprepared for them.

The best way to deal with these moments is to know they will come and face them head on; with them to be ready for anything and know we may need someone to help us. This may sound easy in writing, but this can be harder in real life than we think. For myself, I was always doing everything for my girls and getting them the help they needed. When it came to my ability to ask for help, I was rather stubborn and even unaware of what I needed to do to be ready for all situations. It took me a long time to get the help I needed and some ridiculously hard lessons along the way. Sometimes, I gave up and took a break by stopping my emotions and just walking through the process.

This is one reason my family struggled at times when they should not have. I did not realize how I hurt my girls and marriage because of my resistance to getting help. I hope you can have fewer bumps and be more prepared for them. That the "what if" thoughts will not be able to stop you from being the support your child needs. When they have their "what if" moments, you will be able to help them because you are ready to.

We do not blame them for our financial, emotional, and personal issues. We take responsibility for our decisions and our mistakes. We need to be honest with where we are, and if these doubts may have been attributed to these situations, I was unaware of how much these doubts caused me to not do something for my children when I needed to. I allowed others to cause me to doubt my decisions. I had to face myself. When you don't blame others, you are dealing with yourself.

You will have financial issues when you have a child with special needs. These will come due to medical issues, school or psychologists. When you do know that there are options, you will not blame your child. Raising a child is not cheap. The cost is worth every penny when you know your child is safe and sound and receiving everything they need. Emotionally, the cost is from you and how you can deal with the stress that comes from everyday needs.

As parents, we give our love and support without thought to our children. This comes at a cost. My Pastor, Christine Woods, always reminds us that we must take care of ourselves so we can be there for others. A Pastor gives and takes care of the people in their congregation without holding back. My Pastor and her husband, Bishop Lester Woods, show unconditional love to each of us. They show us how to take care of ourselves and still be there for our children and others in our lives. I am here to say when you hold back from your child emotionally, it hurts you and your child.

Each of us has personal issues. As couples, we have disagreements, and sometimes, we split up. I know this because I did it, and I was married and divorced three times. Other issues can be a bad day or just not sure what you are doing is right. We know our issues are ours and learn to see beyond them to the answers. Because our children are not responsible for the issues, we should protect them and see that they are there for us to take care of and not blame. The "what if" moments lead us to blame our children, spouse, job, parents, and sometimes life for all our problems.

I remember a time I blamed everybody, including my daughters, for what was happening. My marriage was falling apart, and my husband was emotionally abusive. He would call me dumb and tell me I was lower than dirt. He treated me with no respect and said I was no good because I did not have a degree. I believed him and decided that was why I was not doing the best I could. This feeling crept into my work and how I fought for my kids. I felt my opinion did not matter, and this stopped me from helping my kids, and I blamed my husband so much for everything. I learned that everything I did was for me to stand up and say I am worth more than anyone can say.

Blaming my husband, even with the hurtful words and emotional abuse, only made me hurt my kids because I held back from them, which stopped me from giving them the help they needed at times. Blaming something else can be blaming your job for not having enough time with your child. If we are honest, we choose to use our time in other areas. There are times when we need to put something off and put them first. They need to know that they are your joy, not the reason your life is not what you want it to be. This is not easy. In fact it is downright hard. We, as parents, live our lives through our children in one way or another. We tell ourselves we don't, but we do.

The main way we do this is the way we see the world. We see the wonder of the world in their innocent eyes. Some of us put expectations on them that are not realistic because we want them to achieve them for our sake. Children with special needs may never be able to complete the goals we want them to achieve for physical or mental reasons. As parents, we must realize that we may need to care for them into adulthood. I am an example of this. I help each of my girls in different areas. It may only be a drive, help with a bill, or just be there to listen.

My girls can take care of themselves physically and take care of medical issues. They do need me in ways that mean my time is not my own when I need it to be. I may give up my plans, but I find that when I do, most times, it is worth it. What we give up for our children is given back to us so much more. You may have a child who will need physical help to get up in the morning or go throughout the day. You may feel like you are giving up so much, but remember what you are given in return with every hug, kiss, and I love you that your children say with their eyes and words.

Another way you may have to help your child is financially. For Carolyn, I had to be the payee (the person in charge of the finances for another person). Due to some not so wise decisions on my daughter's part with her finances and running out of money within days of getting her monthly check, I had to take over. This meant she had so much a week to spend, and I paid for the rest, including groceries. She had to ask permission to buy anything over a certain amount. As a parent, you want your child to be able to be independent, and yet I was doing everything for her again.

I had to train her how to take over her finances. I also had to let her know she had not failed and to learn from the experience and to see that it was okay. Most of all, do not blame your child for having to do these things because they are innocent and doing all they can every day. We need to be grateful for every day, no matter what it has for us. When we can see the little things as big as our little angels' beautiful faces, we can celebrate them even better when the big things happen. This does not allow the diagnosis to define the child and stops us from truly loving our angels the way they are meant to be loved.

Another thing we do not want to do is blame them for our lives being different than we planned or wanted. We are adults, and we make our decisions about where we go. If we have these beautiful babies who needs us to take care of them, we should not be blaming them that we cannot go out with our friends every weekend or achieve the academic goals we have. These "what if" times are important to overcome. You cannot keep asking yourself, "If I weren't raising a child with special needs or any child, would I be where I am?". God puts us where he needs us to be. We must quit doubting, learn to say what we must do, and learn everything we can to help these innocent lives.

As parents, we must realize that the dreams we started with when we were young don't always have to be forgotten. Our children are given to us to make our lives better and more fulfilling. What does that mean in realistic terms in everyday life? Well, that means you can be an example for your children by working to fulfill those dreams. For myself, I gave up the college money I had through the army. I had been paying into a college account with the army, where they matched with five dollars. When my oldest was just a few months old, my husband and I went through a very tough financial time.

We discussed our options and decided to cash in my college fund. I remember saying one day, I will go to school. As time went by, the dream became dimmer and dimmer. I worked so my husband could go to college. I was to go after he graduated. My daughters seemed to need me more, so I put it off. I finally can look to fulfill my dream because I have been blessed with a job that helps their employees and encourages them to go as far as they want. Yes, it is several years later, as my oldest is about to turn 35, but I am working towards it now. This is just one of many dreams you can achieve. You can start your own business or even write a book.

What are your dreams? What have you thought you would never be able to do? Your challenge is not to look at your child as a barrier but as a reason to try harder to achieve your goals. It is easy to blame those around you for not achieving your dreams. I have blamed my family for not having enough time to work on this book. As in every family, we have a lot of things going on in three different households.

I felt I could not work on this book when I lost my mother. I allowed myself to put off what was important to me, not these situations. Though I had a loss, I also gained because of remembering how much I learned from my mom and seeing how my children are becoming more independent. I hope you can learn to see blaming your children for not getting that job, traveling the world, getting that degree, or being able to do whatever you think is so important is just a way not to face how to achieve these goals.

What we need to learn is our children's "what if" moments. They have them every day. We need to see what they are showing us and hear what they are saying. Sometimes, this can be hard, especially if they are young. This is where we must learn how to read the actions and expressions of our children, not just what they say. As parents, we can get into our own "what if" moments. We need to realize that behind those smiles and sparkling eyes are moments that can be very confusing and leave your child wondering, "Why am I here?".

"What if" moments can come in many different forms? This can be a look of feeling lost, inability to explain what is going on, just wanting to be held, or lack of interest. As parents, we need to be able to look past our doubts to see theirs. Taking time to talk to them and find out what they are feeling is essential for all ages. One of the best ways to do this is to be at their level and make it easy for them to talk. Letting them know they have a safe place to go and be honest with what was going on. Our homes should be a haven full of love and where we can say what is on our hearts. We never stop learning what we need to do to help them.

You will find a new challenge in reading their "what if" moments at every age. When we think we know our kids well, we must remember that children are full of surprises. How they express themselves may not change, but they can learn to hide what is happening. My oldest and middle daughter were great at this when they became teens. Both were having issues that I did not see. Both girls hid within their symptoms as they worsened over time. I tried to help but did not know anything until we were at the doctor's. I was so unprepared, even after years of raising my girls.

You can never get the feeling that you have it all figured out. There is so much to learn each day. Sometimes, it is us that we need to deal with. We are our own worst enemies. We cause the blocks that stop us from learning our children's what-if moments. These moments range from a bad day at school to feeling unsure how they fit in this world. You are the person God has given your children to help them learn where they fit in this world. We need to know it isn't just us having doubts but our innocent children, too. Being able to say sorry is important, and learning from our mistakes is important. This way, when we have those "what-if "moments, we can see where we began and how far we have come.

In my experience, my children went from one diagnosis to a more severe diagnosis. I would see things getting worse and yet not know if I was imagining the episodes or what I heard them telling me what they were going through. I was in denial of what was going on, and another "what if" moment would come. I would think, why did I let this happen, or did I feel I failed my children? Sometimes, I went into a depression and emotionally was not there for my children. I had to get back up, apologize to my girls, and begin again.

These experiences I have gone through on my own. "What if" moments have taught me that without them, I would not be who I am? Every "what-if" moment I learned from brought me closer to being the best parent for my girls I could be. The main thing I want you to know is you will have these moments. How you deal with them will affect your child and their feelings about themselves. I know this because my girls have all had issues with their confidence in their lives. I look back at how my life was in chaos and turmoil because of my not dealing with them correctly more than once. But I never gave up, and even now, I continue to tell them they are beautiful, strong, brilliant, and amazing young ladies.

Please understand you are your child's number one fan, no matter what they are going through. When your child has those "what-if" moments, be there and help them know it is ok to not have the answers. Tell your children they are amazing, are not alone, and can do anything they want. Show them that some "what-if" moments can lead to amazing discoveries as well. I hope you take the time to learn your "what-if" moments and how to go past them to be there for your child. In these moments, we can be the parents to show them that these challenges cannot stop them from being the amazing adults they are meant to be. "What if" moments are challenges for all of us. Let us help our children feel loved and know that no matter what comes, they can face the "what if" moments and confidently come out better than before.

I have explained "what-if" moments, but now I want to tell you how to face them and learn from them. First, you realize and acknowledge that you are having them. This is hard because we do not want to admit we are not the experts and have it all together. I was once told by a mentor to my second daughter during a particularly hard time that I was being a great example of strength because I kept trying and never allowed the things happening in my life to stop me.

I was learning in front of her how to grow and change instead of running away from the challenges. Here I was, living in a rented room with my children, with either their father (Bobbie), in a friend's home (Carrie) by her own choice, or in a college dorm. I felt like I had failed my children. I lost my home and was working an exceptionally low-paying job. "Who was I,?" I thought. I had to acknowledge those what-if moments and realize I could overcome them. Do you know your "what if" moments? We all have them. We must acknowledge them and realize what they are.

After you realize and acknowledge the "what-if "moments, you will need to decide if you will allow this moment to stop you from being the parent you need to be. That means you need to face it head-on. Please do not put it to the side because it will grow and become even bigger than it already is. I have learned how to face the "what if" moments from the especially important people in my life, including my daughter.

These people range from my Bishop Lester Woods Jr and Pastor Christine Vincent-Woods to my mother, who faced the biggest "what-if" moment in her life when facing cancer. My children taught me through the way they faced their own "what if" moments. What I learned is you cannot run away from them. This does not mean you face them alone.

In some moments, you will need your support group, and in some, you will not. The fact is, face it and decide who will win, you or the what-if moment. I want to say I always won, but I cannot. I would like to think I won more than I lost.

After you decide who will win, be strategic. I heard many messages while in church about this. We should be strategic in our lives in every area. What does this mean? It means to have a plan. How are you going to face and defeat these moments? Where are you going to get help if needed? What are you going to say? How long do you have to complete your plan? Some "what if" moments only need a thought, and others need some research and time. The other thing you should do is let someone know who you trust and what is going on. They can keep you accountable and encourage you.

During the process of raising my daughters, I had to have certain people keep me accountable. My mother was a great support in my life, always encouraging me but always telling me the truth. She kept me accountable for everything I asked her to. Do you have a friend, family, or someone close to you who will be there to help you plan and stay with the plan until it is completed? This can be more research on your child's diagnosis or current situation.

This could also be you making some changes in your thinking and how you approach the situation. No matter what it is, be strategic. Now, if you have decided that the if moment has won, well, there isn't anything to do but allow the "what if" moment to grow bigger. If it is bigger, it will take even more to defeat it. I learned this the hard way. By ignoring symptoms or the what if moment of my daughter getting worse, I was faced with a situation where I had to put my daughter in the psychiatric ward in the hospital for 3 days. As a parent, I promise you that you do not want to face this.

I was told once that as a parent, you take on the challenges you mean to win. That means you don't have to win if it is not vitally important. If you can allow some give and take in certain situations. An example is if your child wants to sleep on the couch instead of the bed and it is safe, then let them. Now, if it is unsafe, you would need to work with your child to get to bed: You will have to judge how to do that.

One thing you must know if you start dealing with something is to be prepared to finish it. If you tell your child it is not important to deal with, they will think they are unimportant. The other end of that is known if you are getting out of control and may go too far. You need to know your limit as well. Sometimes, we just have to say, "I will be back."

A good example is when your child cries and will not stop, and you can't take it anymore. If you can safely put the child down, get someone to help you, or leave the child for a few minutes (if old enough), then go and calm down. After you calm down, go back and see how you help your child.

It is better to get some space than say something you regret later or do something worse. I advise you to evaluate each situation and decide if you need to win or allow your child some room to grow and become dependent on their choices and mistakes. When you evaluate the situation, you will decide the best way to deal with it.

Once you have completed these steps, you will find that some results may not be what you want. If this happens, try a new way to face it. You must be versatile in your approach because every moment requires a different way to face it. It may take you asking someone else who has experience. The most important lesson I learned is to assess each moment and do what it requires me to do. Just like children, no two moments are the same. No two "what-if" moments are the same, either.

We must be ready to evaluate each "what-if" moment as a new one. There are times when it seems we deal with the same issue every day, but it is a new situation. What caused the situation may be something different. An example of this is a bad day; someone said something that hurt, or they may not feel well. The goal of every parent is to see each situation as new so that we can make sure we are seeing our child's needs. I hope you have learned what you need to do in these "what-if" moments. Take the moments one at a time. You can do this and be the parent and help your child through their what-if moments.

3

⌇

Deal With Yourself

Now that you have seen that it is ok to have doubts and these "what-if" moments, I want you to see yourself. In our church, we are learning about self-awareness. I wish I could have learned these years ago. What does this mean? It means to be aware of how you think, feel, respond, and talk to others. Why is this so important? It is because if you are talking to your spouse, friend, boss, and especially children in a bad way, you are hurting your relationship with them. Have you ever asked your spouse to do something, and they just give you a look or say something sarcastic back to you? Have you said something to your supervisor and said the right thing but in a bad way?

You go away, hitting your head and saying why did I do that. I feel that I am the worst in these situations, but I am learning every day to improve how I speak to others. One thing we don't think about is how we say our words. It is so important to think before we say something. Are you listening to how you say things or when you say things? Every day, we need to be aware of how we talk. The way we speak can leave a lasting impression on our children and those around us. Listening to yourself is a very important part of that.

How do you become self-aware? You honestly look at the man/woman in the mirror. What are you like? Are you grumpy, lazy, motivated, loving, or stubborn? It took me several years to truly get a good picture of myself. I was a scared woman who did what was needed but never had confidence in herself. I was too afraid, to be honest. I could not say "no" to the people around me. I was a fierce warrior for my children but did not care for myself. I was not able to quit when I felt alone. I was suicidal at times, but my children were depending on me.

Then I saw how I cared for people all my life, and I was needed not just by my children but those who were in my life for the right reasons. When I realized I was more than the words told me to tear me down, I learned to love myself. I learned to say I was beautiful and could do whatever I needed to for me and my family. I learned how to allow those who were bad for me out of my life and cling to those who were there to love and support me. I learned how to forgive myself for all my mistakes. This was hard for me because I had to be real and acknowledge that I did things that hurt me and my family, especially my children. I wanted to help them, and sometimes I failed. This helped me see how I spoke and carried myself.

When I began to have a relationship with God, I had to see how I had been running from many things. I write this book as a mother who has made many mistakes but learned how to overcome them. The first step is being self-aware. What came out of that was a bumpy journey to where I am now. I see myself as a woman of God who is here to help those who need it in many ways and to love others even when they do not love themselves. What does that mean? That means I am there to help all those whom God has put in my life to help them when they are lost or just having a cloudy day, encouraging them when they are struggling, and sometimes having to give the hard talks when needed.

Knowing who I am helps me be there for my children when they need my support, guidance, understanding, and unconditional love in times of challenges. Though my children are grown, they are still my children facing challenges with their diagnosis and the stresses of daily life. Even with the help of all the medical and psychological assistance, a mother and father's love is essential for a child with mental or physical challenges.

In my mother's last years, I was there to take care of her through cancer and dementia. I had to be the person to show love even when she could not. The same is true for my children. Being self-aware is for more than just yourself. It is for every person in your life. It is the best example for your child. For this reason, I urge you to learn who you are so you can be everything your child needs you to be.

How does this pertain to helping your child through their bumpy journey? My Bishop Lester Woods Jr. put it best. When I deal with me, and you deal with me, we can help each other. Now, our children are learning from you how to deal with their emotions, doubts, and even how they see themselves. Do you love yourself enough to take care of yourself? Taking care of yourself means more than physically and out-wardly. It also means your spiritual or emotional self. When we deal with ourselves, we change what needs to be changed, be honest with where we are in situations, know when we need help, and investigate who is best to help us. When our children see us taking care of ourselves, they learn to care for themselves.

When we deal with ourselves and come together, we can help each other. If you are so busy dealing with everyone else and never deal with what is going on in your life, you will get lost and not be able to help others. Think of it this way: if the only thing you talk about and think about is your children, what others are going through, or how you can fix everything for everyone, you will find you will lose who you are. I have had many conversations with my best friend Petina. She will ask me what I have done for myself lately. I usually will say I am doing something small. When I do, she will remind me to take time for me.

I have used my kids, marriages, jobs, and any other reason I could find to not take care of myself and do something just for me. Now that my girls are older and my mother is no longer here for me to care for, I have no excuses. I had to learn what I needed and loved all over again. Being a mother and caring for my mother was a wonderful way to use my time. But it took me time to see how I had run on empty many times. Our children need us to be there through the easy and hard times. When we get overwhelmed by life and do not deal with things in our lives, we check out and cannot love our children and support them completely. We are not only hurting our children, but we are also showing them that they are not an important part of our lives.

I understand this very well. When my children were young, I would get depressed to the point of emotionally shutting down. If you watched me, I was doing it all like a robot. I would say all the right things but with no emotions. When my children needed to be hugged or encouraged, I was there. You would see no caring or concern if you could see beyond the look. These times would not usually last long. I began seeing therapists when my children were young. I never did so consistently, though. Looking back, I wish I would have so I would have been there more for my children.

I hope you will deal with yourself so you can help your children. You can show them that they can love themselves and others. Taking care of yourself is not selfish, as I used to tell myself. It is one of the most important things you can do. If you don't, you will run out of what you need. It is called being burned out. Then how can you love and care for your child? Being able to say "no" is okay. You also need to know how to take care of yourself while not taking care of your family and those in your life who need you. This can be friends, co-workers, or clients. There is a line you need to have to keep in perspective the needs of others and your needs so that they are both met.

Taking care of yourself should not take away from the care of your family emotionally, financially, or spiritually. What do I mean by limits? That is, are you spending more money on your needs than the family, are you spending more time alone or doing what you want with your friends than with your children and spouse, or do you only think about what you need and not what your family needs? Recently, I was at Walmart and was walking by something my mother always wanted or needed, and I began to think about her. I wanted to get it for her, but since she passed, I could not. I cannot tell you how often I will find more for my children who do not live with me but do not need me to buy them because they can themselves.

My oldest daughter tells me to think about what I want. When she does, I get back to thinking about what I came to the store for. When you put your needs and wants before your family's needs more often than you put them before you, look at yourself and see if you have crossed that line. If so, it is up to you to adjust your behavior and find the line in your life. Being self aware and taking care of yourself does not mean thinking only about yourself, but keeping you ready for what is happening in your family now and in the future and helping your child through what is happening in their life.

As a parent, we need to know our choices are for the best of us and those we care for. Our child may not even understand why we are choosing certain things. Making sure we are doing what is best for ourselves so we can be fully there for our children who may be feeling unsure helps them to see that they are important to you and that they can do the same and be there for others. When done right, your child will not realize anything except that you are always there and that they always feel loved no matter what happens.

This is the reason we need to see who we are and how we need to take care of ourselves. This can be getting a massage to seeing a therapist. For myself, I have learned small things like a walk to clear my head, cleaning when upset, listening to music, helping someone else, getting my nails done, and now writing this book. When Ginny and Carrie were in school, I would work out and take a walk when I wasn't working. This helped me get myself in a calmer state of mind. As time went by, I added different things, like spending time with God in prayer and reading His word, sewing, and spending time with my friends.

The one lesson I did not learn until later was consistently doing these things. I hope you will learn the importance of taking consistent time for yourself. This can be like a date you have with just yourself. During the day, we set time for others and give them our full attention. We also need to set some time aside for us and do something we enjoy. What do you need to take care of yourself? Be honest with what you need. You need to know boundaries and not cross them. Respect the boundaries. I want you to see that if you constantly put everyone else in front of you,

you will 'burn out and become emotionless and unable to be with your children like they need you to be.

I know I learned this lesson the hard way. My children suffered through too many times of that. I cannot take those times back. I hope you can see how you are needed, and when you are not there, your children are lost and alone. This may sound harsh, but it is true. It is okay to take some time for yourself so the rest of the time, you can be there for your children. You can set specific times, but be flexible because life can throw a few curve balls. When you are setting a time, make sure you set your priorities. You do need to take care of yourself, but not at the expense of your family. There is a balance you will need to keep as well.

Speaking to a therapist is immensely helpful. I have many times, and it has helped me through some incredibly hard times. Over the years, I have gone to therapy with many different issues. Some of these issues were with the children, and some were with other relationships. Having a child with special needs can cause a strain not only in your every day but also in your other relationships. Due to this strain, you may need family and personal therapy. There are times when telling a professional can be easier than telling a family member.

One thing I have noticed with my girls, and I believe with all children, it is easier to talk to someone other than their parents. I have seen my daughter tell her therapist a deep, dark secret after I left the room when she was young. She was afraid to hurt me or that she would be in trouble. The therapist explained this to me when I would go in later. Some things I was told, others I was not. My daughter decided if I could be told. This is also true with their friends as well. They can tell them things they cannot tell me. Therefore, family therapy is good if you can do it so the child can learn to talk to you about what is happening in their lives.

Unfortunately, in my family, I could not get my whole family in therapy together. I did work with my daughters in every way I could to help my daughters. When you need a therapist, remember to show yourself as real and honest with the situation. You may not get all the help you need if you are not. Always investigate all options when looking into therapists. Some specialize in areas that can help you.

Each person has a different way of dealing with what life has given us. For that reason, the therapist should fit your specific needs as well. An example is, at one time, I was seeing a Christian therapist. This helped me at the time because I was trying to get through a hard time without medicine and wanted to focus on a spiritual way to deal with my depression as well as how to be better in every area. Some may want a more clinical approach to therapy or an alternative way to deal with what is happening in their life. Make sure the person you choose is right for you.

Another aspect of becoming more aware of who you are is knowing how to accept where you are and forgiving yourself for your learning experiences. Some would call them mistakes or bad decisions, but no matter what you call them, they are stepping stones for your growth as a person, parent, and spouse. Being able to look at yourself and say you forgive yourself will also help you convey that to others. From there, you can start the small steps to better communicate with your spouse, supervisor, and child, no matter what is going on.

This is important, especially with your child, because when they see you changing, they know they can too. When you can love yourself honestly, you can show your child unconditional love. Then, they can learn to love themselves through the challenges. That is what they need at any age. I see it in my daughters in small ways. I live with my oldest daughter, and sometimes, I get agitated with her OCD. She cannot help some things she does, yet they can get to be too much. When this happens, I can shut down and get rather annoyed with her. This is not right; I should be more understanding. Knowing this is becoming self-aware of what causes my responses and can help me change my response. This way, I can be prepared for the next time and respond differently. After 35 years, you would think I had this all figured out.

One thing Ginny does is offer to make dinner for me (she loves to cook and show her love that way) or will go out of her way to do something for me. My inability to convey what I am thinking lovingly causes her to wonder if everything is all right and how she can fix it. As a parent, we should be the ones setting the example. Knowing yourself also means knowing when to use tough love and do it lovingly. The first step is knowing ourselves inside and out and whatever is not helping us or those around us and actively changing.

We need to learn how to communicate to our children. It is okay to not be perfect, but we should keep working at being better every day. This means being honest with who we are and growing into being the best parents for the child who needs us in every way. As we approach each day, forgive yourself for the mistakes you make. Do not hold what is imperfect against you, but know you are a work in progress. You work to be the best you can be and allow yourself to be human. Do not put such high expectations that you constantly see yourself as messing up. Be real and honest with yourself, but give yourself and others a break and see you are only human. Forgive yourself first so you can forgive others.

I have told you the ways you communicate, but I want to give you some practical ways in which you can communicate with your child. One of the best ways is to look them in the eyes at their level. You don't want to tower over them because that can cause fear and anxiety. Even if you are saying something loving, if they are seeing you frustrated or rushed, they may not hear it that way. It only takes a few more minutes to pick up or lean down to your child and show them they have your full attention. This also shows they are being listened to as well. Being at your child's level shows them that they are important and that you understand them.

When you show them this and speak to them in love, you show them that they are worth more than words can say. It builds their confidence and helps them see themselves as worthy of your time and love. To a child who hears many mean words from children their age, or a society that says if you are not perfect, you are not important, tells them that they are not smart, beautiful, or wonderful, they need to have that communication to counteract these messages. They need you to look them in the eye to say the bad messages are wrong, and they are more than a diagnosis.

When you are self-aware, you will be able to make time for your child and convey to them that they are very loved and important to you. Allow the love to come through the way you look at them, talk to them, and show them how to live the best life they can. I hope the practical ways of seeing who you are, taking care of yourself, and effectively communicating with your child will help you see what you need to do. What if you need help to become self-aware and learn how to truly take care of yourself so you can be the parent you need to be? You will have the plan and be able to carry it out. I want you to know that this journey is a lifetime, and you do not have to hurry through it. Take all the time you need. Do what you need to do with the purpose of becoming that parent your child needs you to be.

4

Communication

The most important part of any relationship is being able to communicate with those around you. This includes your family, those you work with, supervisors, friends, and everyone you contact.

Communication can be verbal or body language. The look on your face can speak a thousand words. Have you ever watched someone walk into work and you know they are not having a great morning? We all do the same thing. Some can cover all emotions and have a poker face. You do not want to play poker with these people because they never show any signs of what their cards are.

In a way, life is sort of like poker. We are dealt a hand, and we must know how to play it, know what cards to discard and what to keep, and hope the new cards are going to work with the cards we have. This does not always happen. When we are given this perfect-looking child, we do not know what the future holds for certain. We can plan, but do not know for sure. When the bumps come, we will begin to show them in our faces, voice, or body language. Even the poker face people cannot hold it forever. They will break eventually.

This is one of the main reasons communication is so important. We need to learn how to communicate effectively. For some, this comes extremely easy, yet for those who it does not, this can cause a great challenge. Communication is something that can be learned. One story that shows this is one my Bishop shares about himself. He struggled with stuttering as a child. He could not hold a conversation because of it. If you heard one of his messages, you would not be able to see any of what he went through. He has a way of communicating with those whom he speaks so confidently and concisely with what he is sharing.

We can have a disability that is not visible that can cause us to stumble. We must learn how to improve the way we communicate, as well as sometimes expand the ways we communicate. I am an example of writing my feelings down easier than saying the words. Others communicate through their actions because they do not know how to put into words what they need to say. A great example is when someone hurts someone else but cannot say "I am sorry," but instead, they will buy gifts or do something for them. Each child with a disability must learn for themselves the best way to communicate. One of the responsibilities of a parent is to help them in this as well as learn to be better communicators. We need to help them learn their special way of communicating. Every person has a way of communicating. We need to help our children learn what works for them. We will look at different ways to communicate.

One way we communicate is verbally. This is how you say a word is important as what you say. If you tell your child or spouse, I love you, but you say it like you do not mean it, they will have a hard time receiving it. I remember when I was young, before I had children and got married, I wanted to be loved and did not believe anyone could love me because I did not love myself. When I would tell my mother I loved her, I would do it like a quick comment. There was not much meaning behind it, the way I said it. My mom never really said anything about how I sounded.

Looking back at the time I did that, I can see I did not know what those words meant. When I graduated high school, I joined the Army. The saying that you don't know what you have until it is gone is true. I remember calling my mom from basic training and just being so glad to hear her voice. It made me feel safe and like all would be well. That is when I realized the words "I Love You" meant something. Every time I was about to get off the call, I made sure I told my mother I loved her with a different tone and meaning. I ensured my mother knew I genuinely loved her in my voice and how I said it.

We take for granted how we say something. We cannot hear our voices; even if we intend to come across one way, they can sound different. When we talk to children, is our tone loving? Are we using the best words for the situation? When you ask your children to do something, are you barking orders or giving directions in a loving voice? I know we are not perfect and will say something in the wrong way. The catch is stopping before it happens again. The fact is we need to check ourselves and be honest with how we are speaking.

My profession is phone work; dealing with people who need help with stressful issues in their lives and need direction, answers, options, and sometimes just to vent. I must be able to convey with confidence the answers and sometimes just listen to them. One of the main lessons we are taught is to smile when you talk because it shows in your tone. The same with children who are unsure how to put things into words. Parents need to remember our children do not always mean to sound angry, confused, or unsure of how to say something. There will be days they are just having a bad day and say something meant to be loving, and it comes out rather abruptly or as if they don't care.

This is when we need to use our communication skills to find out why and be understanding and forgiving. You need to speak to your child and let them know you are sorry. Talk to them at their level and tell them why you are sorry and that it is not their fault. I have had to relearn this recently with my grandson Dominic. He is 5 years old and diagnosed with a medium level of autism. When he is hyperactive and accidentally aggressive towards others, if we react without thinking, he will get upset and run away, curling up and hiding in a corner as if he has done something horrible. As a grandmother, I feel like I have failed to help him. Instead of judging what he does, we need to guide him and show him the correct behavior and reaction.

If we are honest, our verbal communication can be one of the areas we need to look at before we speak. My mother has told me more than once in my life, "Think before you say what you are about to say." This usually happened when I was angry and was about to say something. But there were times when she would tell me when she knew I had something to deal with and did not know how to convey it. I can hear it in the back of my mind even now when I am talking to someone. We are not always able to do this. When this happens, be honest with yourself and the other person.

One of the hardest things to learn is to say, "I am sorry," and mean it unless we are in touch with who we are and what we are doing. Those times when we are having a stressful day, and our child, spouse, mother, or father comes in and asks us something or says something that does not agree with us, let us stop and remember they are not the source of your stress. If we can just stop acting do not react to the comment, we can save a fight, hurt feelings or our child feeling as if they are unloved. The goal as parents is never to have our children feel anything but love and that they are the best gift that God could ever give us. This should not end with our children, but with everyone we deem important in our lives. I hope you will be more careful how you say things and ensure the tone is appropriate for the situation.

Another aspect of verbal communication is when we do not talk lovingly, we can cause emotional damage. In my family, we were yellers and did not discipline properly. My mother spanked me maybe three times in my life. Instead of disciplining me, she would yell at me. She did not know any different. That was the way she was brought up. This did not help me as a child without a disability. I felt like I could not please my mother for a long time. As I grew up, my mother and I were able to work through those emotions and grow closer in the right way.

I swore I would not be a yeller when I became a mother. Unfortunately, I did not break the curse. I am not proud of it, and I pray that my children will break this cycle. I have seen my daughter do the same thing with my grandson. I have tried to help her by saying I was wrong, but it is a lesson one must learn on their own. One thing my daughter has learned since my grandson was diagnosed with autism is that this will exasperate the situation into a meltdown for him. She is learning how to deal with situations differently. This is one thing as a parent, we must be willing to learn a better way. I am sorry I did not until my kids were older. I hope you can learn what works best for your child. Once you learn the best method, use it properly and never stop learning.

Being honest with how you say things, not just what you say, is one of the most important things to do when dealing with a child who already has challenges. How you speak to them will decide how they will look at themselves. If you yell at them, they will feel like they are not loved. If you say you love them, but your voice shows frustration or anger, they will not know you genuinely love them. If you are having a bad day, you are telling them they are a bother even if you do not mean to, which is what they will believe.

I am the worst of all in this area. I try hard to speak lovingly, but it doesn't always happen. I must ask for forgiveness when I do not. I have realized that not saying things the right way or yelling instead of talking is a form of emotional abuse. I realized when dealing with my mother, who was getting to the latter part of her dementia, how words said in anger or frustration can hurt even when you are 50-plus years old. When you hit someone physically and hurt them, the body will heal. When you say something in the wrong way, those words stay around for a long time, some forever.

I know that I was emotionally abused, and even though I have been able to go forward, those voices are there in times of doubt or fear. I have learned to say go away to them. They can no longer hurt me, but it took years of healing and forgiving the person. My children have told me they forgive me for all the times I failed in this area. I had to forgive myself. I hope this helps you see how your words affect others, especially your child. When you look at your child, remember what you say is meant to build them up. Please consider what you say so that you don't tear them down. I was once told for every negative remark, you should have ten positive remarks. This is a goal we should all strive for.

How you walk, stand, and hold your head shows so much about you. I will describe two people walking into a room to show you how body language can show a lot about you. The first person walks in and is standing tall with confidence. They have a smile on their face and are comfortable in the room. People begin coming up and talking to them even though they do not know them. They visibly enjoy the environment, and by the end of the night, they know everybody.

The second person becomes visibly nervous. They look tense and scared and do not show any signs of wanting to speak to other people in the room. They go into a corner and hide so no one will see them. The other guests who see them are not quite sure if they should speak to her. Due to not knowing what to do, they stay away and leave the person in the corner. What a difference between these two. The first person is my father and sister. They can go anywhere and make a friend. They can speak to anyone and put them at ease. The second person is me, especially when I was younger. I am better but still not the best in big crowds. I showed these examples to show that the way you carry yourself, whether at home, work, or in public, shows a lot about you.

I bet you are wondering how body language affects your child with a challenge of their own, whether physical or mental. If you are always nervous around your child and scared to be a parent, then they are in this alone. They will know if you show your anger through your body language when interacting with your child. They will not know love but anger and fear. If you always show you are too busy because you cannot stop what you are doing, they will feel like they are a burden, and you won't want to spend time with them. If you never look your child in the eye when you talk to them, they will feel like you don't want to talk to them. That other people are things are more important. This will lead to confidence issues in the future.

You do not have to hit a child to cause damage that can take years to overcome. What do you do when you walk into the room, and your family is home? Do you hug your children or say something to them to let them know you see them there? If you do as I stated earlier, I hope it is in love and in a way that you know you are glad to be home with them. Do you walk in like a drill sergeant, ready to get the soldiers in shape? Do you walk in and ignore them completely because you had a bad day or because you do not want to deal with anyone?

These different body languages will receive different responses. If you continue in this behavior where your child feels you do not love them or they are afraid of you. It will show in many areas. For you and your child, this can cause issues that can take years to get through. A child deserves love and all the support a parent and family can give, whether they have a challenge or not. How they see your actions can determine whether they are confident or insecure. A child with challenges can be more sensitive than we can understand. That is why we need to be more aware of how we approach and respond to our children.

Therefore, you need to watch your body language. When your child faces all kinds of challenges from school and within themselves, they need to know that when they are home, they are loved. That home is a haven of peace and love. The way you carry yourself at home will affect that. Practically, this means you must check yourself. If you are married, you must work together to help each other daily in this area. We need to be able to look at ourselves and how we are coming into a room; others are seeing us when we are communicating with them.

Often, we do not realize how we come across. I heard a friend say that after years of being told how people responded to her, she had to look at herself and realize what she was doing. That is why we must be open to others when they tell us what we cannot see. Sometimes, we must talk to people we trust and ask how we are seen. When you do this, make sure you have a person who will be honest with you and not just say what you want to hear. If you do, be ready to hear something you may not want to hear and learn from the person. Also, learn from it so you can change the way you carry yourself. When you do, the way your family sees you changes. They will see how much you want to do the best for you and your family. This will help them make changes when facing challenges requiring change.

The main thing I hope you see is how you interact with your children matters. I want you to think about it from their point of view. Children see parents as examples for their lives. Be that example even when you fail. Let them know that it is okay to make mistakes if you learn from them. Depending on what challenge your child is dealing with, they will be more sensitive to your body language as well. These facts mean we must be better each day and never give up on showing them love and encouragement.

When you walk into a room, others can read your face. Your facial expressions are especially important. When I was young, I could always tell what kind of day my mother had by the look on her face. If she came in not looking at anyone directly, she was tired and did not want to talk. If she came in with that glare look, she had the worst day, and one wrong word would end in being screamed at. If she came in with a smile and a more relaxed face, she had a good day. Isn't it amazing how one look can say so much?

In comparison, my stepfather could tell a story and never show any emotion. His poker face could hide the trick he was pulling or a serious situation. When he said something, we would always look at him and wonder if he was making up something. Does your child have to wonder if you are being honest, or can your love be easily read by your facial expressions? If you are like my stepfather, you may have to put more effort into showing your emotions to your child.

When you speak to your child with these incredible challenges, look at them with love, not anger, frustration, or tiredness. When they think of you, et them think about your smile and the care in your eyes. When you think of your child, I hope you think of their smile and the look of wonderment in their eyes. I always tell my daughter Bobbie when she is having a bad day, "Just look into Dominic's (my grandson) face and see his smile and the love in his eyes." I say that because children have unconditional love and will always show you no matter what is going on, they believe in you.

There were many times when I had such days and did not have the energy to help my daughters. When they hugged me or said they loved me, I knew for them I could go on. This journey is hard, and many walls will come up. But the love of my girls has kept me doing what was needed. Even now, I look at them when times get tough. They encourage me and show me love when I do not deserve it. May you never forget your child is your greatest fan, just as you are their greatest fan. Let the way you approach them show that and not frustration or anger.

As I attempt to help you see yourself and how you communicate with others, body language, and facial expressions, I want you to also watch your child's body language and facial expressions. These are signs of what is happening inside your child's mind and body. It is amazing how someone who knows us well can tell all this about us. As parents, we need to know even more about our children to help them. Sometimes, actions speak louder than words, and we must accurately decipher them to help them.

As our children grow, we need to keep watching as their needs change and the way they show them. Communication is a vital part of all your relationships. I hope that you work on your relationship with your child and actively learn from them how to help them and yourself in the process. The way your child acts shows you what is happening at school, with siblings, and sometimes with the family. The way they think about themselves shows as well. As I advised you about your behavior, the same is true for your child. Look for the times of not having eye contact, how they speak to you, and how they walk into the room.

When I was young, I was bullied greatly, as well as my daughters. My mom taught me to keep encouraging them and giving them time to talk. I also had to learn from the doctors how to help them in ways I was not trained in. With mental illness, stress can cause subtle, noticeably big, and bold symptoms. I learned what body language for each child meant. This may sound easy, but it takes knowing your child. Do you know what it means when your child comes into the room acting a certain way? Be honest if you do not get help from the doctor and whoever has been assigned to help your child. Another way is to read books. Learn all you can to optimize your child's possibilities.

As I have been speaking of different ways to communicate, I have been advising the different ways we communicate. I want to also give you some practical ways to communicate with your child. The first way is to talk to your child at their level. If you always look down on your child, they are more likely to fear you or think you are unhappy with them. Even if your tone and words say the opposite. Going down to their level, sitting down, or lifting them to your level shows them that you have time for them and that you see them. When you reach their level, look them in the eyes and show them they are important.

I would not recommend doing this only when you are frustrated or angry, even if it isn't at the child, because you want to be calm when being this close with your child. If you do so in a moment of anger or frustration, you can scare your child. I am one of those who did, and I had to repair what harm I did. Now, know you will make mistakes, but think about how you talk to your child. How are they seeing you? If you watch their response, you will be able to see it.

The second thing is choosing your words carefully. If you call your child stupid, they will think they are stupid. Your words can build up your child or tear them down. This is in any relationship, but a child who is having mental or physical issues already needs encouragement. There will be times that you will need to correct your child, but do so in love. When you need to correct your child, listen to your child. Every word stays in our minds. We may not remember them all the time, but when a situation comes up, the words come back. Even now, at times, things that were said to me years ago will come back to me Sometimes they are encouraging, sometimes tearing down. Our children need to know we love them, and our words need to show them that. Some examples of what can be used for encouraging words are beautiful, handsome, my angel, gene us, queen, king, lady, or gentleman.

One more thing I would advise you is to check yourself before encountering your child. Do not take it out on your child if you have a bad day. I have many times and regret it. If you cannot get past your day and your child is old enough and can understand, tell them you need a moment before you can be a mom or dad for them. If they are not, push past it and give that child all the attention they need. These innocent children love us even when we are wrong. We need to check how we are approaching and talking to our children. We want them to know it is okay to say I need some time to calm down. If you are having a bad day, take a breath and count to ten if you need to before you go in the house or pick up your child and smile and show them that you are happy to see them.

When our child comes to us saying that they have had a bad day or act like they have had a bad one, we also need to give them the space they need Our children learn how to see their emotions through our example. It is even harder for a child with mental or physical challenges to understand their feeling and how to express them. For this reason, we need to check ourselves every day to make sure our interactions will help them learn from us. Give your child the same room to grow and get through the bad days and learn how to be able to give to others to those around us who need us, as well as be able to just let go of the feeling and make the rest of the day better.

The most important thing I want you to know is communication is vital with your child. They need to know they are loved and that we want them in our lives. They need to know we have their back in every area and will not let anyone hurt them. The way we communicate with them shows them these things. A child who hears or sees things, with a low self-image, and in many ways alone because other children do not understand them, needs a safe place to go. You are your child's safe place. If you are communicating with your child, they have no safe place by your words, face, tone, or looking down on them as if they do not matter, then they are alone. They will suffer because of it. I can tell you that healing takes time. Love your child enough to work daily to help them know they are loved and important.

5

Learn Your Child

I have advised you to become more aware of who you are, but you must also know your child. This means knowing what makes your child sad, happy, or mad. If your child is on medicine, which many are, know the side effects.

We, as parents, want to believe we know our children. The sad truth is we do not know as much as we think we do. This is one area we must work on every day. The reason it is so important is we cannot help our children without knowing what they need.

How can we teach our children? There are many ways, but the one main factor is us. We must actively learn about our children at every stage. The first way is to watch them. When we bring our new baby home, they can't talk. They make these cute and really loud noises, but they can't say what they need in words. We must watch how they look at us and respond to their surroundings. We learn how they like to be held. Some like to be held next to our skin, while others like to be laid on our legs looking up at us. Some babies (all my girls and my grandson) want to be held all the time, while some are okay with laying in the crib or play mat. Some are very loud, and some are quiet.

What do we learn from these observations? We learn that if they act differently, there may be something wrong. When my oldest was a baby, she always cried unless she got held. One day, she was crying, and I picked her up, and she continued to cry. I was a new mom and did not know what to do. I did not have any family near me, so I was scared. I tried everything I knew to do. Finally, I called the doctor, and they gave me the things to check and how to help her. I learned that day how a baby with gas pains can be very painful and uncomfortable for my newborn. I also learned how to help her by patting her back while laying her on my lap face down. This is something small but especially important. It seems the small things are the most important because they tell us what is going on. My middle child would get upset over the smallest thing when she was a baby. If I moved my hand a certain way, she would start to cry. This, I learned, would help me in the future as she got older. What have you noticed about your child? This would be the same if you cared for an elderly family member. This would show if dementia or whatever illness they have is getting worse or if they never show signs of illness, an illness may be detected.

At each stage, each child will show different behaviors as well as if anything from the outside is affecting them. When your child is being harassed by other children, they will show it in how they act before you hear the words. I was bullied and told I was nothing by other kids because I was not like them. I do not have a mental illness like attention deficit disorder, but I lacked confidence. Because of this, I would keep my emotions inside and hide from certain people. I did not feel safe. Imagine a child with challenges facing more severe bullying than those who do not.

When a child is different, other kids will attack it normally. Some will not, but we know there will be those who will. If I, who had no challenges, ran away from the pain, what would a child with challenges do? That depends on the child. They feel it is more severe, so how they deal with it could be severe, such as cutting themselves, overeating, playing video games, or just hiding from older children. Younger children can have issues with urinating in the bed at night, uncontrollable fits, being sad all the time, or being very clingy. I know I never told my mother once about school. But she knew and would talk to me. She told me I was the smartest kid and prettiest, which was why they were jealous. Though my mother tried, these words did not help me at the time, but later they did. After I became a mother, I told my kids the same thing and realized it was not helping, but I still kept trying, knowing one day it would. I learned to read how they walked and looked at me and how to respond. Each of my girls responded differently. My oldest acted like nothing was going on, but then she would not look me in the eye when I talked to her. That was her way of showing me she was hurt. My middle child would sometimes cry and run to her room and not talk to anyone or have a major tantrum over nothing. My youngest would over-compensate for others who hurt her and go out of her way to act like they were her friends.

As adults, they show signs of stress and problems, some the same and some quite different. Can you look at your new baby and know what is going on just by how they coo or don't coo? If your preschooler comes home, can you see what kind of day they have had without talking to the teacher? We want to believe we can. I can tell you from experience that is not always true. As your child grows, you may see odd actions that you don't understand what they mean. My oldest child went through a stage where she was very possessive at a young age and did not like her things touched. Little did I know that she had obsessive-compulsive disorder. It was mild, but these actions showed the symptoms of this disorder. She also sang when she was nervous or when there was tension between her and her father. This was a symptom of Tourette Syndrome. Yes, it was mild, but it is a tick she has. Honestly, if we look at ourselves, we all have a tick, maybe small. My daughter has a beautiful voice, so we never guessed the reason. We thought she loved singing. One day, we had a teacher who told us that when she took a test, she would sing, which was not good. Due to that, we had to modify how she took a test. Luckily, I had a teacher willing to help. This is just an example of why you must never stop watching your child. The disorders I just mentioned are co-dependents of attention deficit disorder.

When I was a new mother, I never thought these behaviors meant there could be a possible mental disorder. My middle child, (Carrie) had actions that did concern me. She had temper tantrums for no reason.

She would cry and scream if she did not like what she was told. After a time, I realized she was faking to get her way. The not-so-funny thing is sometimes, these fake tantrums would turn into real ones. My husband and I did not realize these actions were signs of a learning disability until she started kindergarten. That was until we learned for years that she had been showing us signs of a condition that would be life-changing. Even in preschool, we did not realize it. Another thing Carrie would do is need my attention in everything she did. Looking back at this, I can see she was going through so much mentally that she needed me to encourage, help, and show her that all was okay. In the moment, I did not see what was truly happening. Some children need encouragement and do not have mental challenges. But for those with these challenges, these actions speak more than words could. Every day, we need to be actively listening to our children.

As parents, we must be able to look at our children and know if something is off with them. They need us to be able to help them even when they don't know they need it. We need to be able to see through the physical, mental, and emotional signs. A physical sign can be feeling extra tired or not hungry. These are some physical things you can see. A young child may not know how to say they feel sick. We need to have the observations to see that. They may have emotional needs like how to deal with a loss, being bullied, or just having their feelings hurt.

A parent's goal is to protect them from being hurt, but we know this will happen. That is when we help our child heal emotionally. How we learn that is by learning their responses to these situations. This could be a look, drooping their shoulders, running to their room, or just being quiet. One way they learn these responses is from us, so if we watch our children, we may also learn about ourselves. In this way, we can teach our children how to react in a better way. But it begins with us watching them so we can know how to help them in the best way.

We need to know the child's normal behavior before we can see the changes in any area. For example, is your child hyperactive normally? If so, when they are just sitting, there not wanting to move, then you know something is wrong. Some behaviors you may notice:

1. Not making eye contact with you or others: When a child does not make eye contact, it can be a sign of several things. One can be they are scared by your behavior. Maybe they had a bad day and came home and began talking in a loud tone or just sounding angry. We need to make sure our tone is not hurting our very sensitive children. This can also mean that they have had a bad day. Maybe someone said something hurtful to them at school, and they are sad. We need to notice the little things in everyday life because it is the little things that give the biggest clue. When we see this, we need to see how we can help them. This will depend on the age of the child. A younger child may need a hug and be told it is going to be okay and that you love them. An older child may need to talk about and need more time. We need to be able to give that time.

2. Getting angry easily: We as adults know when we get angry easily, it usually means that we are at the edge and need time to cool off and re-centered. It may mean we must talk to someone or just let go of what happened. The same thing goes for our children. They have a lot of stress every day that we do not see. We may not see the reason. As parents, we are great examples of this. We try to do so much that stress becomes normal in our lives. One thing we do not think about is it will get too much at some point. The same for our children. When we get angry, we are at that point. There are some adults and children who have anger issues. That is something that will need to be dealt with differently. But if your child is having a moment and acting angry for no reason, you would need to investigate why. This means you would need to ask what is happening and help them calm down. This means you need to stay calm. You may need to look at your child's day and see if you need to remove anything so they are less stressed. You must also examine if you, as a parent, are expecting too much. For example, we all want our children to do well in school. We need to help them in every way, but if your child is not an A student due to being unable to learn at the speed needed and getting a C instead, then we need to celebrate them. If they need help, we need to get them help.

3. Avoiding certain situations: Imagine you come home, and your child

is avoiding a topic like their report card. Many of us have done this when we were kids. We did not want our parents to see our grades. Our children may have certain situations they want to avoid that may need more help than we are aware of. If your child is avoiding certain things, places, or topics, you need to look at what has happened. Has your child fought with a friend and does not want to see them? If so, then we need to help them to find a solution. If children are avoiding certain places, they may fear that place, or if they are like my girls, they may have seen something or heard a voice there. My girls saw and heard things that did not exist much earlier than I figured out. I remember when Carrie was younger, we lived in a house where she kept seeing and hearing animals. We found out the previous owner was a veterinarian. She would refuse to go into certain areas at times. When I asked her why, she told me I had to understand where she was and get help for her. So, watch if your child is avoiding something so that you can help them after you find out why. If you cannot get them to tell you, watch and listen to your child. They will eventually show you.

4. No longer taking care of themselves physically: This is for older children more than younger kids. My daughter Virginia did not show any issues with mental illness until she was 21 years old. One day, I noticed she had not had a bath for 5 days. When I spoke to her, I noticed she was not responding as usual. At the time, I did not think it could be any mental illness. I had to find out when she was so far gone that she needed serious help. During this time, I was not able to find help immediately, but when I did, we got the professional assistance she needed to be able to get what she needed. This can be in other areas, such as not wanting to exercise, eating, dressing, or taking medicine. If you see changes in these areas, it may be a sign that something is happening with them. They may be trying to hide something physically, like someone hurting them or them hurting themselves. A sign of mental illness can be hurting themselves. This could also be a sign of struggling with self-image with the challenges they face. When a child has mental challenges, it is hard to get an image of themselves without the challenge being in front of them and them thinking that is who they are. Not caring for

physical needs is a way of acting out and asking for help. When a child ceases taking medicine at any age, it can be a sign they don't think they need it. When your child is young, you can have some control and get them to take the medicine. When your child is older, this can be a challenge. I have had my oldest and middle daughter stop taking their medicine. When they did that, they were placed in a hospital for a different amount of time to get back to where they needed to be and even got the dosage changed due to growth. The hardest of these times was when my middle daughter, as a teenager, went to a friend's house and stated she was going to go home and stab me and kill me. Fortunately, her friend's mother was a nurse and gave her the option of going to the hospital or she would have to call the police. My daughter stated she would go to the hospital. I discovered she was putting the medicine somewhere in her room when it was given to her. We can only do the best we can. We as parents need to be able to see the signs and do all we can to help them.

5. A child reverts to a previous behavior: When our children reach certain marks in their lives, they should continue to go forward. For example, once your child is potty trained, they should not go back. Sometimes, they do for several reasons. It can be they want attention, sometimes a physical issue, or they can be confused by something that is out of their control, like something they may have seen or heard around them. Outside forces can cause a child to return to something comfortable, where they feel safe. This can be sucking their thumb, talking in baby talk, wanting to go somewhere they used to go, or being with someone who may not be around anymore for many reasons. When this happens, we need to investigate what has happened lately. Taking time to talk to your child is important to get their point of view. We need to help with reason before we help them to go forward again. We might need to get help from others. Sometimes children find talking to other people than their parents much easier. We need to be open to help when it comes to helping our children.

Another area we must learn about our children and their actions is how medicine affects them. All medicines have side effects. When our children have challenges, mental or physical doctors will prescribe medicines. They will warn us about side effects but tell us not to worry. As a parent, we need to know each medicine and all the side effects and be willing to tell the doctor that we do not agree with our child receiving that medicine. How we know if these medicines are effective is by watching how our children respond. Does your child act out of control or rebound after the dosage wears off?

Do they have difficulty with their daily needs? Are they not eating, able to respond to you when you tell them, acting unusual, or having physical problems? We need to know this to help our children and be willing to tell the doctor they are not working. If the doctor is unwilling to seek other options, be willing to look for another doctor. One job we need to take seriously is being our child's advocate in all areas, especially in this area. When my middle child had a doctor who kept giving medicines to counteract certain medicines that were not necessary, I told the doctor I would not agree to the changes. I requested a new psychiatrist when I was told I had no choice. When that happened, we were given the best choice for my daughter, and he changed her medicines. When that happened, a lot of the concerns that I had were gone due to fewer reactions to deal with. Also, the severity of the reactions was lessened.

I know it is hard, but be able to be the advocate your child needs. One of the ways you can learn about the medicines your child is taking is by getting a book about medicines and their side effects. Due to being a certified nurse's aide during the time for seventeen years, I was fortunate to have access to one of these books as well as medical information from the nurses that I worked with. These books gave me the information I needed when talking to doctors and to know what to look for in my child's behaviors.

Ask questions when talking to your child's doctor using the information you learn from the book. Write them down so you will not forget them. Also, take notes when you are getting the answers from the doctors. This shows them you are serious about advocating for your child. They may even offer to give you written instructions or information about what they are advising you. When you are being advised on a new medication, ask questions and write down what to look for. We all forget things or can fail to see things when they are not on our minds. I know for myself writing down things solidifies that in my mind. You need to do what works for you. You may also want to put a note on the refrigerator to help you. When you see something that the doctor needs to know about, writing that down helps you remember when speaking to the doctor.

I know this sounds like something that is rather basic, but the most basic thing can be the most important. If any severe change happens after adding a new medicine or dosage, let the doctor know immediately. With Carrie, I had to do this due to several changes and several reactions that, to me, were severe. After talking to the doctor most times, I found that these reactions were not nearly as bad as they seemed. In some instances, though, I was told to bring my daughter in to see the doctor. There were times when the medicine was changed. Therefore, I emphasize this because we can get comfortable thinking medicine will fix things. This is not correct.

I have always told my daughters that medicine is ten percent of the answer. The other ninety percent is in their mind. We do not make notes just when new medicines are used or changes in dosage. We also watch to see if a medicine is no longer effective. If we see that the benefit of the medicine is wearing off, we need to take notes to see if we need to change the dosage or get a new medication. If they can no longer function as they used to, we must be aware and let the doctor know. Some signs to look for include lack of focus, appetite increases or lessening depending on the medication, not responding to you or situations like they used to, being more tired or wired than usual, or grades suffering (if in school). These are just a few signs you may see that would make you need to talk to the doctor. When speaking to the doctor, be specific about the things that concern you.

The second way to learn about your child is to listen to them. What is your child saying to you? Are they saying they need more attention or things to make them happy? Are they saying that someone is hurting them with words or actions? Is that person that is hurting you? Are they saying they are afraid of you? Are they saying they need you because you are too busy for them? What are the words they say, and how are they showing you? These are particularly important questions because they tell us how we need to respond. If you listen carefully and focus fully on your child, you will hear what they convey to you. In this world where we have at least ten different things going on at once, it is easy to get caught up in what is happening around you and not give your child your full focus. As parents, we don't want to think we give our kids less than we are. Let's be honest, we all have done it. That is why I say to focus on your child when they come to you and say, "Mom, can I talk to you?" or just comes to you and needs to say, "I love you." As parents, we usually think our child wants to do something. I know even now, when my grown daughters tell me they love me, I still do the same thing. Sometimes, they just need you. When you show you are listening, they will know you are listening, and then you may hear them. The best part of this process is you begin to really hear your child and learn where they are and what is going on in their mind. Sometimes, they don't say what will interest you and show what you need to hear. What is between the lines and words can say volumes. If your child is not talking about school, then there could be issues at school. If they only want to talk about one thing, then this can be an area of interest in which you can help your child expand.

I was talking to a friend on the phone not very long ago, and she reminded me how easy it is not to say what is happening. She asked how I was doing, and my response was okay. She then asked me how I was doing because I always say that. Then, we had a conversation about what was going on in my life. We must do the same thing with our kids. We ask them, "How was school?" and they say, "Okay." Children with mental challenges do not easily share their feelings because they do not know how they feel. We must ask questions to find out. When you actively listen to these answers, you discover what your child is going through. In each stage of your child's life, you will need to learn the cues that they need you. I found my kids need me even at 35, 32, and 23. They have different ways to say it. When I was taking care of my mother, I found times when my mom would do the same thing. She would get upset if we did not spend enough time together. This was when her dementia was worsening. I learned from that day my mother needed me more, and I had to make changes. Every day, you will learn something new if you listen to your child and all the people in your life. Listen to the tone your child is using. The tone your child or you use is important to show what is happening behind the words. Different tones show different feelings that we are going through. Some of the tones you can hear:

Low monotone; This tone can show different things. The most common feeling it shows is boredom. They are not interested in what you are saying and more than likely not listening. This can also show tiredness. When a person gets so tired, it comes out in our tone. When you suspect this is the issue, let your child know they can get some rest, and then you can talk later. Tiredness comes in different ways. You can be mentally tired and cannot handle any more information. They need to process what they have been given and then can deal with new information. They can be physically tired and need to sleep. We get so busy we do not rest when we should. Our children do the same thing. When our kids are younger, they do not want to go to sleep but may be so physically tired they cannot handle it. We all have been there with our babies, rocking them to sleep when they are fighting it. Our teenagers stay up talking to their friends as late as they can. Sometimes, we need to deal with the issue later when they are rested.

High pitch; This can mean different things as well. One of the things is excitement over something that is going on. We need to encourage them to do what makes them excited. This can help them be able to build self-confidence or friendships. We need to be excited about them. This can also mean joy in the moment. A good example of this is Christmas morning. Our children get so happy about presents and all that comes with it. We need to see the joy in everything so our children can see the same joy.

Deep tone: This tone can mean anger or not wanting to show. When your child does not know how to deal with anger, they may come to you and try to talk to you. They may respond in this tone if they don't want to talk. We need to be able to identify this and help them express their anger in a good way. This means we may have to put our feelings aside, especially if our child is very young and cannot speak it. We need to know when we cannot help our child as well. Sometimes, our children need to speak to another person, such as a therapist. If we can assess the situation to see what we need to do.

Hesitation: This is a sign of anxiety, doubt, concern, or fear. We need to be great detectives and read the signs. The tone is just one part of the equation. Look what has been happening with your child. Is there anything in their words to go with the tone? The best way to find out is to ask your child if they can tell you. Be as loving as possible in this situation because our challenged children are very sensitive. This is a situation where you must treat our children with special care. When a child comes to you with any of these feelings, most of the time, they do not know how to express them. We help them learn by showing them how we do it with our feelings, as well as reaching out to them and allowing them to be real with us. How we do these changes as the stages of their lives change. As parents, we need to learn to help them at each stage.

The third way you can learn about your child is by listening to those around your child. This can be other adults, brothers, sisters, parents, the parents of friends, psychiatrists, therapists, and teachers. Then, some may have experience with children who share the same challenges your child has. I was part of a support group when my daughters were just diagnosed. That experience taught me how to listen and what to look for in their behavior. I learned that even though every child is different, they go through most of the same challenges. One of the examples is a child with attention deficit disorder will have one or two areas they really excel in and can put all their focus on. As a parent, I was encouraged to watch for that area, and because of that, I learned that Carrie was interested in animals to the point she learned all she could. As an adult, she loves animals and has a heart for animals. She has a cat of her own as an emotional support animal. As a parent, I encouraged this by helping her get the information she wanted. Since we had a dog, she helped me take care of her. You need other points of view because they can see things you cannot. Sometimes, we are blinded due to being too close to our child.

Have you ever had someone tell you something about your child that you did not see, like they were being extremely aggressive or they were acting odd that day? This should prompt you to look at your child and attempt to see what is going on with your child. When you do, you may find out from your child it is nothing, or it may be something you can talk out. One thing I would emphasize is to consider the source or the observation as well. Some sources do not know your child well enough to give input on your child. My grandson is in preschool, and we have had more than one report of him being aggressive. We had to look at why. The reason was the way he played with his father and uncle. The changes were made to not play in the same way. Since these modifications, the reports have been less since then. My grandson is still aggressive at times. Now we are aware of what can cause this and have lessened this behavior even more.

Learning your child is a lifetime job. Being a parent is a lifetime job. As the years go by, you see different stages in life. At each stage, you must relearn what is best for your child. The challenges will change as well. The challenges at 5 years old will not be the same at 10 years old. Even when they are adults, the challenges change if the season in their life changes. My middle daughter had her first child sixteen months ago, and prior to that, she had never even changed a diaper. I was there when she first got married and had to help her and her new husband through some tough things. This is a new challenge both for her and for me. During the last sixteen months, I must help with several things that I never thought I would have to. I have listened to her during each phase to see how to help. The hard thing to learn is some things are out of my hands and convey to her. As a parent, we want to make everything easy for our children, but we cannot. Now, I will learn how to help her through this new challenge. My daughter has matured in many ways, and I know she will be a great mother. I will be there for her when she needs me and be watching to see what I need to see that she cannot tell me. Our commitment to our attention does not end; the support level will never change. I hope you never stop learning about your child, no matter how old or hard they make it. We cannot give up on them because they will give up on themselves if we do.

For those taking care of family members who may be older or with disabilities, know that the same goes for you. You must listen to them to see the changes. Watch them during each phase of their life to know how to help them. The difference is it may be where their illness is progressing. I encourage them to take in each moment and be grateful, even in the hard times. When the person no longer needs you, you will miss that person so much. I know because when I was caring for my mother, she was not having an easy time. We had many times when I was blamed for what was happening. When I had to take her to the hospital for medical reasons out of our control, that was the last time I saw her for almost a month. My mother went through so much, and I could not help her. I could not listen to her and find out how to help her. Until the end, I did everything to help and show her I love her. I wanted to listen to the words, body language, and how they conveyed what they were saying. Every day will be a challenge, but the best reward is to love people through what life is bringing to them.

6

ᔰᔩ

Learn All You Can About the Diagnosis Your Child is Challenged With

To say; "Learn about what the diagnosis your child has been given," is an understatement. The best way to help your child is to know what they are facing. The words stated by the doctor are big and sound very overwhelming. When you learn what they mean, it can be even scarier. My Bishop is always teaching that education is so important in the word of God and whatever you are dealing with in your life. His wife, Pastor Christine Woods, has taught us about mental health. She reminds us that we need to do what we can to have great mental health.

Part of that is learning about what we are going through and going to the professionals when needed. The same goes for our children who are facing a great unknown with this diagnosis over their heads. Learning more about each big word and breaking it down so you can understand is as much for you as for your child. It will show you the signs and possibilities that they will face. This also includes the elderly and those who may not be children in your life. Understanding what the challenge is gives you the ability to defeat the challenges coming.

I went straight to the library and got every book I could. I learned that attention deficit disorder always has a codependent. They range from Bipolar to Schizoaffective. That means if they have that diagnosis, they will eventually show signs of something else. The level of the co-dependent can be extraordinarily low or extreme. They can change, as my middle daughter experienced. Her diagnosis went from ADD to Attention Deficit Hyperactive Disorder to Bipolar (when she began seeing things that were not there) to Schizoaffective.

When she was diagnosed with attention deficit, I learned that her mind is like a train that keeps changing tracks. That is why she sometimes cannot concentrate on one thing exceedingly long. As an adult, she still has issues but is better. As she grew older, she began to have other symptoms. Then, the diagnosis changed. I had to learn about each new diagnosis and medications that went with them and how they would affect her challenges. The challenge was being able to understand the information that was given to me. Therefore, we must learn all we can in the way we learn best and from what helps us the best. The books I read gave some important information, but this was just the beginning. I had to, and you will as a parent as well, go from reading to actions and putting the information we learned into action. Start practicing what we learned.

How can you break down the big words and use them to help your child? Well, these days, there are more ways to do research. You have the internet. There are so many points of view and fact-based sites on the internet. Take the time to investigate all that you can. Look at the symptoms of the challenge. That way, you can know what your child is going through. I had to do more research when Carrie had an episode where she believed she had spiders in her mouth and was afraid to talk or close her mouth. At this time, she was diagnosed with bipolar disorder. This was the beginning of new challenges due to new symptoms and medicine. For that reason, you will never stop learning about some form of the diagnosis.

You will find new information referencing what you are facing on the internet. I encourage you not to just rely on the internet, though, because the information given is from that person's point of view. Therefore, I advise you to take the information and see if it will help you understand what you seek to learn. Learning the definition does not mean you understand the disorder. When doing your internet research, look for all the information to break it down so you can digest it and put it into words you can say to your child. Using a resource such as the internet can help you see the positives and negatives of the diagnosis. If we can see the good and bad, then we can show our children that some parts of their lives may not be so great the amazing parts of their lives outweigh the bad.

Another source is books. Yes, read a book and take notes; if you own it, highlight or underline what is important to know. Some books are nothing but science and words that may overwhelm you. When you get one of these books, I recommend getting all you can out of it and not allowing the parts you do not understand to stop you. What you do is ask someone who can help you understand. I will be referring to that later in this chapter.

Read more than one book. I read books about diets, experimental medical options, how to raise a child with certain issues, what causes these disorders, and a few books that advised practical ways to help my daughters. With every book, I took notes and tried what I thought would help. Some of the things I tried did help while others did not help. You will need to find what will help your child. Every child is special and has individual needs, whether having a diagnosis or mental challenges. I do not use the word disorder because using that word can make a child feel like they are damaged.

They are made special by God to show us true love in many ways. Many books I read only seemed to show my daughters as damaged. I hope you will never see your child or convey to your child that they are damaged. Be careful what you take from the books you read. Looking at a book as a resource is good, but do not allow it to change your view of your child.

Remember to see your child as a gift from God, not a diagnosis given by man writing a book. Sometimes, we get into the words so much we forget we are dealing with a child.

Talk to the professionals that God has given you. Ask as many questions as you need. Do not be afraid or intimated by the doctor. If the doctor is unwilling to truly help you and your child, do not be afraid to find another doctor. Be willing to get the best doctor for your child. I was lucky I had the best for a couple of years to have a doctor who turned the corner for my daughter. He helped my daughter not only improve but thrive during the time he was her psychiatrist. When he left us, we were very sad to see him go.

When you have someone who helps your child, you want to keep them on your team if possible. Sometimes, we need to change it up to see other options as well. If you do the same thing every time, it does not mean it will be the best idea. Another professional who can give great help is your child's therapist. They can break down what is possible and what to look for. I hope you get the help you need from the professionals in your child's medical team. They are a great source of information. When you have a great therapist, you can get the best help for your child.

Make sure whoever you get to help your child is the best for your child and family. A therapist can make a big difference. They can reach your child on different levels and in ways a parent cannot. We had an amazing therapist for Carrie. She was able to show me how to communicate with Carrie and reach her. I was able to get Carrie to open up to me because of that. Your family should be involved in the care as well. They should be able to get ideas to help your child. The only way to help your child is as a team.

Another great source of information about your child is support groups. You can find these groups online or in person (when available). You learn from other parents' new ideas on how to help your child in all types of situations and ages. Also, you learn how to help yourself by seeing how other parents deal with stress. This is where you can get a chance to be real about your experience and get feedback from those who have been through it.

There are many types of groups to investigate. When considering a group, research it to make sure it will fit your situation. The areas of concern are age group, type of diagnosis for the children, and the area in which it is. If you do find one that looks interesting, try communicating via email with the person of contact. I recommend asking questions about the group. We want to find the best fit for our children and us. Do not be afraid to try something new. The best support group for you is your decision, but be careful when choosing. Safety is especially important for you and your child.

When you feel you have learned all you need, I want you to remember that learning never ends. When you feel like you have arrived, start at the beginning. When you feel you have reached the end, start back at step number one. We, as parents, never reach the end of the journey. My mom told me no matter how old I am, I will always be her baby. I tell my daughters the same. You may not need to read as many books, but keep up on it. With each step, you have new information to help your child and yourself.

This research will help you keep your emotions and mind in check as well because you will be prepared for what is to come as much as you can. I have not mentioned that when you do all of this and make mistakes, as we all do, know your child is watching and learning from you. They will learn to not just give up because of a challenge that looks overwhelming. They will learn that when you face a challenge, no matter how long the word is or how big the mountain looks, you climb it one day at a time.

Today, my oldest daughter and I were talking, and she said that the process of raising a child with special needs is up and down. The child forgives those bad days and remembers the good days. This is from a child who has lived with mental challenges her whole life in one form or another. Looking from your child's point of view is hard sometimes. I hope that you realize your best resource is your child. They can share what you are doing and where you need help. Research is not just about the diagnosis; it is also about the way your child thinks. No amount of internet research, book reading, or professional insight can tell you exactly how your child is feeling or what they are thinking. I hope you will always go to the best source, your child.

7

~

Basic Training

When you think of basic training, you think of the military. I was in the US Army, so I know a little about basic training. I want to tell you a little about basic training in the Army. First thing when you arrive, you have no idea what you are in for. Most of the time, the recruiter lied to you to get you to sign up. Once you get there, you are learning things so fast your head spins. You must learn skills that you may not have even thought of. Physically, mentally, and emotionally challenged, you have a drill sergeant barking orders and demanding you listen even if you are ready to pass out from tiredness. When you think you figured out something, you find out you don't. You learn who you can trust and who is out to cause you harm.

Now, the one thing you learn is how to respect others and the time given to you. You learn how to organize your time and when to reach out for help. One of the things you learn that will get you through is how not to quit. If you made it through all twelve weeks of basic training, you have grown as a person in every way and are prepared for the new lessons that will come. You are taught to have goals to reach each day so that you can complete the course you are on. So, how does this come close to parenting? Well, we need to have the same attitude to never quit, and the things you learn can help you as a parent.

I learned discipline and what real respect is. I bet you are wondering what his and raising a child with special needs have in common. There are a few things they have in common. The first is discipline in our lives. When I say this, I mean that we as parents must be disciplined to do all that God has given us to do. Our lives are remarkably busy, and we can get overwhelmed by our schedules. This means our children can get lost in the shuffle. How can we get discipline in our lives? We must make the decision to work on it every day.

The way we do this depends on what our demands are. The basics in completing this is to make a schedule with goals for each day, where you can make time for your child and still complete all other requirements. Be versatile and learn not all the things you have on your to-do list will be done in one day. Know your priorities and make sure your child knows they are a priority. As parents, we will miss some things, but if you miss every meeting or show, then they will feel as if they are not important to you. It takes self-discipline to get up and do what is needed and not give in to the feeling of 'I cannot do this.' It is easier to say 'I cannot do' than 'I can.' In basic training, we are given a set schedule and goals to achieve each day. When making your schedule, ensure the goals you must complete at that time for you and your child. You may even want to schedule your child if you need to.

Some days, I would get up and feel like I could not do it today. I remember the days of basic training and how I had to push myself to face the day. This may sound strange when comparing raising a child to basic training. In a way, being a parent of special needs is a training day every day. We must plan to do what is needed every day. One main factor is staying focused on what God has given us. The most important thing we are given is our children. Because of all that can happen, we face the challenge of keeping priorities in mind.

In basic training, we have different areas where we must learn to pass, if not excel. Some instructors guide us in their own way. Along the way, we have challenges that seem overwhelming and can scare us. We are left with this feeling of wanting to run and hide. I cannot say how many times I felt this way. I have always been told I was stubborn and persistent. That is how I got through my time in basic training. I learned to be tough and yet more understanding when situations came up. I feel this helped me in helping my children.

How do we translate this to raising a child with special challenges? To be a parent of any child, we need to be organized, disciplined and never accept defeat. When in basic training, you learn how to face your challenges, accept help, and push yourself every day, even when you feel like you want to quit. You also have a drill sergeant who pushes you and helps you achieve what you never thought you could do. That drill sergeant is your child.

First, you must realize that from the day your child comes into this world, you are no longer alone. You have now become part of a family that will require being there for each other. When you join the real military, you become part of a big family. You have your crazy cousins uncles, as well as your brothers and sisters. I was told a story when I first joined, and that was proven later with the U.S. Army.

The story goes that a group of Army and Marine soldiers were in a bar. One of the Army and Marines got into a verbal fight. The other soldiers became aware of this, and on both sides, they backed their soldiers. Now, for my experience, when I was traveling home one time for the Christmas season, I was approached by a person and was extremely uncomfortable. Within a few minutes, a fellow Army soldier sat next to me and said, "He was sorry he was late, and was I ready to get something to eat?" I was so relieved that I responded yes, and we left. When we got a little way away, he told me, "We soldiers are family, and we protect each other.

The reason I state this is not only is this translated into how we physically, mentally, and spiritually help our children, but we also need to protect our children in every way. Let me start with how to put these thoughts into practice. When in basic training, the first thing to do is get a schedule. I am sure you are saying you do, and most of the time, you cannot do it all. Some can, but they wear themselves thin and will eventually burn out. So, how do you get a schedule that works?

The secret is to keep trying until you get there and be willing to change if necessary. There are requirements for each family. When you have a child with special needs, you have more requirements due to what challenges you face. This means your schedule can comprise more doctor appointments, therapists, or organizations that can help you. On top of that, there is work, time to have fun with your children, and, if you are married or in a relationship, time with your other half. This sounds exhausting already. You are even busier if you are active in your church, going to school, or involved in any type of organization. There are many examples of people who do this every day.

Honestly, I tried awfully hard in the beginning and failed many times, but eventually, I got the schedule where I could do this. The first thing to do is write down what you need to do. Then, prioritize what needs to be done. One thing I did was put in writing the appointments and my work schedule and then my husband's schedule when they were young and not in school. At first, I was overwhelmed to the point of convincing myself I could not do this. Then I prayed about it and decided I would get up every day and get done all I could. Some days, my house did not get done perfectly, but my girls had everything they needed.

One thing I learned was to be versatile because nothing was written in stone. Our schedule is written in pencil. With all these possible changes, we still need to have a schedule on which we base our day. This allows us to train our child who has schedule challenges to learn how to set a schedule. We set the example like the drill sergeant does for the soldiers. After you write down what is needed, be real with yourself and be willing to say I cannot do this. This is hard because we want to believe that we can do everything. Be willing to ask for help. That is your spouse, mother, father, and friend. It takes a village to raise a child. It takes a battalion to complete a mission. We need to be honest with where we are in life and what our needs are. As our children grow up, the schedule will change as their needs change. This process will continue even when they are grown. I am still working on schedules with my daughters to this day. I am blessed to be there for them during every stage. I hope you see that a schedule will help you in beginning this basic training.

Step two is, once you get the schedule, to have the discipline to do what is on it. If you have to work out three days a week before the kids are up, you get up and do it. If that means taking extra time with your child to help them learn a subject in school, make time for them. This is important that you not talk yourself out of doing what is needed each day. It is so easy to allow that voice in our head to say, "I don't have time for this." I know I still do this. We as parents must make time even if that means we change our plans.

This takes discipline to not give in to these thoughts. Discipline does not mean that you will be perfect. It means you get up every day and say I can do this and stick to it. Though it may sound easy to some, to others, it is hard. To follow a plan for the day and not get overwhelmed is a victory for you and your child. How do you do this? You not only decide, but you put into action what you decide. That is, you will get up and do all you need to do to make your child's day a great one. This includes making breakfast, spending time in the morning, and encouraging your child that they can do anything.

To put this in practice every day, think about your day and what is needed. What does this require of you? What do you need to do that may not be your choice? Now comes the decision to do what is needed. Here is where self-discipline comes in. Are you going to complete the task that is needed? Let me give you an example. Let's look at a normal morning. If you wake up late and rush to get dressed for work, make breakfast, help your child get ready if they need help, and then rush to the daycare or school, how does your child feel? They may have a tough day ahead of them and need a few minutes of your time to reassure them and show them that they are loved and your priority.

What do you think is the outcome of being disciplined enough to get up and make the morning time a time for you and your child to talk or just be there to hug them and show them they are loved? They feel encouraged and loved, so when a challenge comes, they know they can face it. This is also seen in how you approach your own life. What your child sees, they will copy. So, if you have no discipline in how you spend your time money, where you go, or who you are with, that is what your child will learn.

Being disciplined does not mean you stay rigid, but you do not allow distractions to stop you. A great example is when it is time for you and your child to spend time reading, which may be difficult for your child, and you get a call from a friend who wants to talk, but you can call back later. What do you do? Do you tell your child you will read later or ask your friend if you can call them back later? This may sound rather a small issue, but when your child needs your help, even in a small way, they need to know you are there for them. This is not always easy. We get tired and need rest. I just want you to know it takes that decision and following through each day to help your child.

The third step is to do the work. What does that mean? That means you get yourself in the battle each day and do all you need to do. You already have it written down and decided to do what is needed. Now, the battle isn't always visible. Sometimes it is behind the scenes. Your child may look perfect outside, but inside is having issues out of their control. How, as a parent, do you know the battles and how to fight them? That is where doing the work comes in. The work is putting into action all you have learned from your research and from watching your child.

How is this about basic training? Well, as a trainee, you are given certain goals to achieve. Just like your child is given goals to achieve in school and daycare. The only difference is in the training. Yes, you are training your child. If they see you do the work, go to appointments, make time for them, train them to do chores, teach them to read, how to cook, or have fun and laugh. That is why you put into practice all that you learn. In this process, you will learn what does and does not work for your child. While training my two oldest children, I read so many books and tried everything I could to see if it would help.

Putting the processes I learned into practice was hard work. In the military, I was taught many new things like shooting a rifle, how to do such physical moves as a male push-up, how to march, how to look up when marching, and, of course, how to follow rules. The Drill Sergeant did the work required to train me to do what I needed. As parents, we are not militarily training our children but in a loving way. But we must put the work in so that we can set an example and show our children how to do it.

I was told when I was younger that it will not be work if you do something you love. If you go by this, then we should not see putting in the work as work because we love our children. I hope you will see that putting into practice what you learn from books, doctors, teachers, and those in your and your child's lives is not work but doing it for love. Also, you will start seeing that putting in the work is vital to helping your child through some tough times. This will help you as well. If you can put the work in for your child, you will see you will do so in your own life. This helps you and your children.

The last thing I want you to learn from basic training is self-respect. Self respect comes from how you see yourself. You are taught in the military to present yourself not only as a representative of the military but also as someone with pride in your appearance. You can indeed tell a military man or woman how they carry themselves. That means we walk with our backs a little straighter, how to walk in step with others, how treat others with respect by saying "Yes, Sir," and show pride in our appearance in how we dress. We must have self-respect so we can train our children to have self-respect.

Life shows us enough challenges as parents, and our children have even more than we can see. When we have self-respect, we do not allow these challenges to overcome us but now face and defeat them. How do we get self-respect? We see ourselves as we are, see what we need to change, and allow us to be human. I have learned in my relationship with God that we are loved and we are special. Because of this, I can see myself and say I love who I am and look forward to who I will become. For many years, I did not allow my daughters to see me make many personal mistakes.

I have learned that being honest with where we are is the first move. That is the same in the military. You are assessed to see where you are so the Drill Sergeant can know where to begin. Well, the same with you in your home with your child. You need to look at yourself and not be afraid to say here I am. As a parent, we need to help our children have the same self respect because so many people try to tear them down. I have always told my children they are amazing and incredible. This may sound basic to many, but it is so important.

8

∿

Conclusion

By this time, I hope you can see a light at the end of the tunnel. When we are given our children, whether they are challenged or not, to love and support in every way. This is a privilege that should never be taken for granted. Sometimes, our children with no special diagnosis can feel left out and that they must take care of their siblings. The truth is no two children are exactly alike. You may not see the differences as easily with all children. My goal was to help parents face something no one can fully prepare for. Whether physical or mental, being told your perfect child has challenges that most adults would give up on is overwhelming. Hopefully, what I have said in this book will help you process the information given to you and see your child as the gift they are.

We always want to start with getting past the diagnosis and seeing your child without it. My daughter advised me of what she was told 'See the person, not the diagnosis." The same goes for a child who has been given a diagnosis. Our children do not know anything but what they have received. For this reason, we need to be able to hear the doctor but not allow what we are told to stop us from pushing forward and helping our children to be the best adults we can be. This starts at the beginning of a child's life.

I hope you have learned a way to process the facts and have the determination to not only help your child but to help them excel beyond what others may say they can do. When we have a child with learning challenges, we should have the ability to see our child doing more and not envision all the struggles they will have. This is a challenge for any parent, but when you know, there are more than the usual challenges. We automatically think of the worst things when we first hear those words.

I hope you can use what I have learned and not allow that to be the only thing you think about. I hope you can get past the "what-if" moments of the situation and say you can do this and be the parent your child needs. The biggest part of that is seeing your child as the perfect gift they are, and you have not been given more than you can deal with. I know you can not only get past that moment of doubt but excel with love for your child.

Make sure you can see yourself and what you must do for your child to help them in all areas. Every parent should know who they are, their strengths and weaknesses. Hopefully, you can see this more clearly and begin to work on your weaknesses. Our children are depending on us to be able to set the example of how to be self-aware. Honestly, this will not take one day but a lifetime journey.

The best way to do this is before you have children, but when our children are given to us, we must be even more honest with ourselves. These what-if moments can cause such doubt, and our defense is to know who we are. When we know who we are, we can help our kids who struggle with self-awareness have the best example to learn from. I know that in my life, I have had to take several moments of where am I that brought me to a place where I could help my daughters.

I hope that in my struggles in this area, you have learned a method that helps you in your situation. What I have dealt with and, in some ways, still dealing with may be different, but the road to deal with them can be the same. I truly believe that we go through things to help other people. I know that you can help others as well once you have gone through these situations.

One main way to help your child is communication. In my previous chapter, I advised the ways to communicate. I am not an expert in any way, but I hope how I explained the ways is a way that you can change how you speak to your child. Knowing how we carry ourselves and react to certain situations will guide us and indicate what we need to modify with our children. Maybe you, as a parent, must start from the beginning with your child and apologize for not being there when you should have been. Maybe you must learn a new way to communicate with your child in the new season of their life or your life. This area of our lives affects every part of our lives, but we never really see how we affect others. Remember that when we talk to our children, let us be at their level, even if that means we need to get on the floor physically and use only small words. We should always see the opportunities given to us to communicate how much we love our children.

We need to learn how to read our children so that we can help them and know what they need from us. I have learned so much about myself from my children. They have kept me going when I wanted to just quit. We learn how to grow and to see life in a new way. When we have children in challenging situations, we learn how to help them and show them how they can help themselves. Let us never stop learning from our children for many reasons. The most important is to see their needs. Look at each way they communicate to you what is happening in their mind, body, and in the season you are in. As your child grows, your resources will change sometimes. Be willing to change with the times.

Hopefully, you are ready for basic training. This training will get you to the place where you can be prepared for the challenge that you are facing. Know that you will get stronger as the days go by and the lessons are learned. Do not be afraid to make mistakes. We learn when we fail and learn the better way to do something. Also, be sure to keep going forward. One step at a time on every new day. You may not have the physical demands of basic training, but the mental is just as difficult. This training will make you the parent you need to be and love your child the way they need you. Never doubt the process, even when it seems impossible. There is a light at the end of the tunnel.

I want you to know that you can do this. You may have been given information that changes everything you ever knew, but know that everything is happening for a reason and that you would not be given a child with a challenging future if you were not equipped for it. This does not mean you will not need help. You will need all the help you can get. As a parent, we must be able to accept all the help given. I hope I have put in more practical terms what you need to know and how to get there.

This book is meant to make your life as a parent of a child with a challenge a little bit easier to understand. Those big words do not have to scare you or make you feel like it is an impossible task. You will have days when you do not want to continue, but know you get the best reward from your little angel when you do. Honestly, being the mother of my three daughters was and still is the most important thing I have ever done. I never take them for granted. I hope you see your children as the angels to make your life the best it can be. I hope what I have said helps in some way. May you have the best life with your child and always see the good in the situation.

About the Author

Lisa McBride

Lisa McBride, a young mother of three children, has faced her share of growing pains and learned from her own mistakes. Inspired by the encouragement of her late mother, she embarked on the journey of writing this book to help others navigate parenthood with grace and resilience.

www.ingramcontent.com/pod-product-compliance
Lightning Source LLC
Chambersburg PA
CBHW051645120626
46551CB00015B/2220